THE CHRISTIAN WOMAN'S

Gratitude Journal

A Prompted Gratitude & Prayer Journal
with Encouraging Devotionals

STACEY A. SHANNON

Welcome!

These pages are designed to help you on your journey of gratitude. You'll find questions to get you thinking, space to write your thoughts, inspirational words, places to keep track of your prayers and more. Use the journal as often as you'd like. Many questions are written from the perspective of evening time, looking back over the day. However, if morning works better for you, just apply the questions to the day before.

Either way, I'm grateful that you're here and hope you find this journal helpful. I would love to hear your feedback. You're welcome to email me at stacey@writtencreations.com or find me on my site, FamiliesWithGrace.com.

Blessings!

Stacey A. Shannon

Date: _______________________________

List three people for whom you're thankful.

1. _______________________________

____

____

2. _______________________________

____

____

3. _______________________________

____

____

What did someone say today that made you happy?

- ◯ Happy
- ◯ Sad
- ◯ Angry
- ◯ Anxious
- ◯ Excited
- ◯ Afraid
- ◯ Lonely
- ◯ Jealous
- ◯ Calm
- ◯ Disgusted

Date: _______________________

<table>
<tr><td>

List three songs you love.

1. _______________________
   ____
   ____

2. _______________________
   ____
   ____

3. _______________________
   ____
   ____

</td><td>

Where did you go today that you enjoyed?

</td></tr>
</table>

- ◯ Happy
- ◯ Sad
- ◯ Angry
- ◯ Anxious
- ◯ Excited
- ◯ Afraid
- ◯ Lonely
- ◯ Jealous
- ◯ Calm
- ◯ Disgusted

Date: _______________________

List three ways you've felt God's love this week.

1. _______________________
   ____
   ____

2. _______________________
   ____

3. _______________________
   ____
   ____

How did you feel God's presence today?

- ○ Happy
- ○ Sad
- ○ Angry
- ○ Anxious
- ○ Excited
- ○ Afraid
- ○ Lonely
- ○ Jealous
- ○ Calm
- ○ Disgusted

Date: _______________________

Life doesn't have to be perfect to be good.

Three Ways to Be Kinder to Yourself

We can all be good at being hard on ourselves and are often our own worst critique. I know I can say some awful things to myself that I'd never say to anyone else. But through the years, I've learned a few ways to help silence that inner negative voice and be kinder to myself.

1. Acknowledge you're doing the best you can.

I tell my children all the time that I only ask them to do the best they can. I've realized I need to ask the same of myself. We can easily start looking around and noticing where we're failing or lacking. But, we also need to acknowledge that we're doing our best.

If you can do better, do so. However, don't get so caught up in thinking about what you haven't done or accomplished that you miss all the things you have. Give yourself grace.

2. Let go of perfection.

Remind yourself that you aren't perfect. I know you *know* that in your head, but keep that in mind as you talk to yourself. The truth is, we often behave and treat ourselves in the opposite way. I get mad at myself for not doing things perfectly. But, I'm not perfect. None of us are. If we were perfect, we wouldn't need Jesus.

I don't want to imagine what life would be like without Jesus. He has seen me through so many things and loved me in ways I don't fully understand. Not being perfect really is OK. His strength is made perfect in our weakness (2 Corinthians 12:9), so maybe our weaknesses are exactly how we showcase His strength.

3. See yourself as others do.

A few years ago, I was a looking at a photo we took on the first day of preschool for my son. I first noticed how frumpy I looked in the photo. Then, I happened to notice my son. He was gazing up at me in love and adoration. He didn't see me as frumpy or notice my faded black Capri pants. He just loved me for who I was.

Take that even a step further and try to see yourself as God sees you. I can tell you that He sees you as His beloved daughter for whom He sent His Son to die. God truly knows you. He knows you aren't perfect and have faults. Yet, He is a loving Father who sees you as a whole person, including all the goodness and strengths you have.

Next time you're being hard on yourself, remember that you are doing the best you can and you aren't perfect. Then take a moment to step back and look at yourself the way those who love you – including your heavenly Father – do!

Date: _______________________________

List three colors that make you happy.

1. _______________________________

____

2. _______________________________

____

3. _______________________________

____

How did you feel love from someone else today?

- ○ Happy
- ○ Sad
- ○ Angry
- ○ Anxious
- ○ Excited
- ○ Afraid
- ○ Lonely
- ○ Jealous
- ○ Calm
- ○ Disgusted

Date: _______________________

List three books you've loved reading.

1. _______________________

____

____

2. _______________________

____

____

3. _______________________

____

____

What made you smile today?

- ◯ Happy
- ◯ Sad
- ◯ Angry
- ◯ Anxious
- ◯ Excited
- ◯ Afraid
- ◯ Lonely
- ◯ Jealous
- ◯ Calm
- ◯ Disgusted

Date: _______________________

List three of your favorite worship songs.

1. _______________________

   ____

   ____

2. _______________________

   ____

   ____

3. _______________________

   ____

   ____

What is your favorite Bible verse and why?

- Happy
- Sad
- Angry
- Anxious
- Excited
- Afraid
- Lonely
- Jealous
- Calm
- Disgusted

Date: ___________________________

Find something in each day that makes you happy.

Understanding God's Love For Us

"Mommy, come!"
"Mommy, come here!"

This is the little voice I hear calling to me most mornings and after nap times. Sometimes my son switches it to call for daddy. And sometimes he gets desperate and just sobs without even calling our names.

When I hear this voice and hear his plea, I go to him. Because he is mine.

We snuggle together to calm his fears. My hair falls over the top of his head and the two intermingle in exactly the same shade of brown. Because he is mine.

We have had our fair share of battles – stubborn ones – throughout his learning to sleep or just to listen when we tell him not to do something. Because he is mine (he comes by his stubbornness fair and square).

At the end of any given day, though, the things I have done for my son and for my daughter are because I love them. They are mine. I see bits of myself in them. My daughter has my sensitive heart and the shape of my fingers. She has my smile. My son has my brown hair and eyes. He has my love for music and snuggles.

I would do anything for them, because they are mine. I don't ignore their pleas for help when they are sick or scared, because they are mine.

How God feels about us
God must feel that way with us. Because we are His, He doesn't ignore us when we cry out to Him. He is there even when we don't realize it. Just like I am never far from my son when he is afraid that I have left for good. I haven't left. And neither does God leave us, even when we can't see Him. God's love for us is constant.

He comes running to us in our time of need because we are His. Whether we can come running and meet Him or whether we need Him to find us in the darkest nights. God is there. He is waiting. He is loving us. Because we are His.

No greater love can be found. I work to wrap my head around God's love and how it can be even greater than my love for my children. It's beyond comprehension, but the glimpses I get make me feel humbled and thankful.

Right now, no matter where you are, no matter what you're facing, wondering or thinking, just call out to God. He will come running to meet you, because you are His.

Date:

<table>
<tr><td>

List Three

List three animals that make you smile.

1.

2.

3.

</td><td>

Question

What made you laugh today?

</td></tr>
</table>

Today's Mood

- ◯ Happy
- ◯ Sad
- ◯ Angry
- ◯ Anxious
- ◯ Excited

- ◯ Afraid
- ◯ Lonely
- ◯ Jealous
- ◯ Calm
- ◯ Disgusted

Prayers

Date: ______________________________________

List three foods you enjoy.

1. ______________________________________

____

2. ______________________________________

____

3. ______________________________________

____

How did you take care of yourself today?

- ( ) Happy
- ( ) Sad
- ( ) Angry
- ( ) Anxious
- ( ) Excited
- ( ) Afraid
- ( ) Lonely
- ( ) Jealous
- ( ) Calm
- ( ) Disgusted

Date: _______________________

List Three

List three of your favorite beverages.

1. _______________________

   ____

2. _______________________

   ____

3. _______________________

   ____

Question

What is something small that made your day better?

Today's Mood

- ◯ Happy
- ◯ Sad
- ◯ Angry
- ◯ Anxious
- ◯ Excited
- ◯ Afraid
- ◯ Lonely
- ◯ Jealous
- ◯ Calm
- ◯ Disgusted

Prayers

Date:

You can never go wrong when
you are counting your blessings.

4 Ways to Connect with God When Life is Busy

1. Utilize alone time in the bathroom.
The most consistent alone time I have is when I'm in the shower and getting ready for the day. So, I use that time to connect with God. It sounds weird to talk about getting spiritual in the bathroom, but it works. Praying in the shower works well for me because I have no distractions or interruptions. I am performing a sort of mindless task and can focus on God more easily.

I usually spend about 10 minutes drying my hair on low with a diffuser (the joys of curly hair!). So, that's when I read my devotion book and Bible then pray over requests on my prayer list I maintain in a free app on my phone.

More recently I've started listening to sermons while I'm getting ready to encourage me as well. And sometimes I add in prayer time while brushing my teeth.

2. Connect with God in the car.
Another great time time to connect with God is in the car. I have used this time to listen to sermons, but what I do mostly is listen to Christian music. Music is powerful and connects me with God more easily than anything else. Listening to Christian music helps me to focus on Him and reminds me of His presence.

Being alone in the car can also be a great time to talk with God (eyes open, of course!).

3. Utilize resources to get into the Word.
I most enjoy using a devotion book along with my Bible reading. I've used a variety of them through the years and do a different once each year. No matter what devotion book you pick, make sure it is focused on the Bible and encourages you to read from the Bible regularly.

I enjoy having my devotion book on my Kindle and use the Kindle app on my phone along with the YouVersion Bible app to read. I love it's all portable, so if I end up getting behind or not having a chance to read during my usual time, I can read anywhere I am when I am able to.

4. Have a verse of the day.
Reading your Bible and delving into God's Word are important to help you connect with God and grow in your spiritual walk. Along with that, I've found having a verse of the day is helpful. You can use a flip calendar, daily Bible app or whatever works best for you.

Scripture cards are also a great way to focus on a verse a day. You can put them in an envelope or attach them with a ring binder clip and rotate through them to keep yourself encouraged and focused on God's Word each day.

Date: ______________________________.

List three of your favorite activities.

1. _______________________________

2. _______________________________

3. _______________________________

Who made your day brighter or easier (or both)?

- ◯ Happy
- ◯ Sad
- ◯ Angry
- ◯ Anxious
- ◯ Excited
- ◯ Afraid
- ◯ Lonely
- ◯ Jealous
- ◯ Calm
- ◯ Disgusted

Date: ___________________________

List three prayers you've seen God answer.

1. ___________________________
   ____
   ____

2. ___________________________
   ____
   ____

3. ___________________________
   ____
   ____

How did you see God's love today?

○ Happy   ○ Afraid

○ Sad   ○ Lonely

○ Angry   ○ Jealous

○ Anxious   ○ Calm

○ Excited   ○ Disgusted

Date: _______________________

List three of your favorite places.

1. _______________________

____

2. _______________________

____

3. _______________________

____

Describe something beautiful you saw today.

- ○ Happy
- ○ Sad
- ○ Angry
- ○ Anxious
- ○ Excited

- ○ Afraid
- ○ Lonely
- ○ Jealous
- ○ Calm
- ○ Disgusted

Date: _______________________

> *Having an attitude of gratitude*
> *leads to a happier you.*

Taking Care of Yourself Matters

"Then, because so many people were coming and going that they did not even have a chance to eat, [Jesus] said to them, "Come with me by yourselves to a quiet place and get some rest." So they went away by themselves in a boat to a solitary place. – Mark 6:31-32

How many times have you started to do something for yourself and gotten interrupted? It happens to everyone, but it especially happens when you have children in the mix. I remember when my children were younger, I wondered if I'd ever get to eat warm food again. Here's what I like about these verses in Mark: Jesus saw that His disciples had a need that was physical. They were hungry and hadn't been able to eat. And He didn't tell them to suck it up because there was ministry to be done. He met their need. He took them away to a quiet place so they could rest and refuel.

The Bible is filled with times that Jesus Himself goes off alone to commune with God and refocus. How much more do we need that time?! It can sometimes seem impossible to get time alone or time to focus on yourself, but you must do that. We need downtime to recharge and refocus. It is hard to focus on God and hear His voice when we are too busy and the world around us (and in our heads) is too noisy.

Finally, taking care of yourself is important because you can't keep pouring into your family from an empty jar. It's not being selfish to take even just 15 minutes of alone time and let everyone else fend for themselves (in a safe and age-appropriate manner, of course) so you can regroup. You will feel better and your family will benefit from that as well.

<u>Put it into practice:</u>
Find a way to have some quiet time today. It may be 15 minutes here and 5 minutes there, but find time. Use it to talk to God. Have real conversations with Him instead of just going through a list of prayer requests. Spend time praising Him and asking Him for refreshment and encouragement. Then come up with something that refreshes you and make it happen within the next 24 hours. It could be 30 minutes spent reading a book, 10 minutes spent polishing your toenails, two hours spent alone at the movie theater or an hour spent wandering through your favorite store.

<u>Bonus Action:</u>
Commit to spending 24 hours without complaining about yourself both in your head and with your voice. Praise yourself for what you're doing well. Focus on the good attributes and successes you have. Turn off the mean voice inside your head that tells you all your faults. God made you and He doesn't make junk, so don't treat yourself like junk!

Date: _______________________

List three of your biggest blessings.

1. _______________________
   ____
   ____

2. _______________________
   ____
   ____

3. _______________________
   ____
   ____

Where and when were you able to spend time with God today?

◯ Happy   ◯ Afraid

◯ Sad   ◯ Lonely

◯ Angry   ◯ Jealous

◯ Anxious   ◯ Calm

◯ Excited   ◯ Disgusted

Date: _______________________

List three of your favorite movies.

1. _______________________

____

____

2. _______________________

____

____

3. _______________________

____

____

What was your favorite part of the day?

- ◯ Happy
- ◯ Sad
- ◯ Angry
- ◯ Anxious
- ◯ Excited
- ◯ Afraid
- ◯ Lonely
- ◯ Jealous
- ◯ Calm
- ◯ Disgusted

Date: _______________________________

List three things you love about your personality.

1. _______________________________

____

____

2. _______________________________

____

3. _______________________________

____

____

How were you able to make someone's life better today?

- ○ Happy
- ○ Sad
- ○ Angry
- ○ Anxious
- ○ Excited
- ○ Afraid
- ○ Lonely
- ○ Jealous
- ○ Calm
- ○ Disgusted

Date: ___________________________

4 Prayers for Women

Strength and endurance

"being strengthened with all power according to his glorious might so that you may have great endurance and patience." – Colossians 1:11

Father, I ask that you strengthen me with all power according to your glorious might so I may have great patience and endurance. Lord, hold me up when I am weak today. Give me strength beyond my own when I'm tired and ready to give up. Help me to keep going until the day is done. In Jesus' name I pray, Amen.

Wisdom and discernment

"If any of you lacks wisdom, you should ask God, who gives generously to all without finding fault, and it will be given to you."– James 1:5

Lord, please give me wisdom as I am raising my children. Help me to discern the best choices for them and for our family. Guide me to know what your will is for me as a mom. Father, help me to be the mom my children need to raise them according to your will and plan for their lives. In Jesus' name I pray, Amen.

Rest and peace

"In peace I will lie down and sleep, for you alone, Lord, make me dwell in safety." – Psalm 4:8

Heavenly Father, I ask you to give me peace to lie down and sleep. Lord, remind me you are always in control and keeping my family and me safe. Grant me your peace that passes all understanding. Hold me close and let me rest fully in you. In Jesus' name I pray, Amen.

Protection and safety

"Have you not put a hedge around him and his household and everything he has? You have blessed the work of his hands, so that his flocks and herds are spread throughout the land." – Job 1:10

Father, I ask that you place a hedge of protection around me and around my family. Protect us in every way, Lord: physically, emotionally and spiritually. Remind me of your presence when I feel afraid. Let me rest in your protection and safety. In Jesus' name I pray, Amen.

Date: _______________________

List three things you can do well.

1. ____________________________

____

____

2. ____________________________

____

____

3. ____________________________

____

____

What challenge(s) did you overcome today?

- Happy
- Sad
- Angry
- Anxious
- Excited

- Afraid
- Lonely
- Jealous
- Calm
- Disgusted

Date: ______________________________

List three ways someone has been kind to you.

1. ______________________________

   ____

2. ______________________________

   ____

3. ______________________________

   ____

What did you eat or drink today that you enjoyed?

○ Happy   ○ Afraid

○ Sad   ○ Lonely

○ Angry   ○ Jealous

○ Anxious   ○ Calm

○ Excited   ○ Disgusted

Date: _______________________

List three reasons you're thankful for God.

1. _______________________

   ____

   ____

2. _______________________

   ____

   ____

3. _______________________

   ____

   ____

What can you praise God for right now?

- ◯ Happy
- ◯ Sad
- ◯ Angry
- ◯ Anxious
- ◯ Excited
- ◯ Afraid
- ◯ Lonely
- ◯ Jealous
- ◯ Calm
- ◯ Disgusted

Date: _______________________________

You are important. You are
special. You are smart.

2 Tools to Help with Anxiety

I've dealt with anxiety throughout my life. There have been easier times with it and harder times. A few years ago, however, it reached a peak. I realized that what I needed most was to see God's goodness. I needed to see what to be thankful for in my life.

Basically, I needed to shift my attitude from the negative to the positive. Life is always going to have negative things, but I didn't have to focus on them. Somehow that had become my habit and was only increasing my anxiety levels.

In an effort to change to seeing the positive things, I started doing two things: praying to see God's goodness in my life and keeping a gratitude journal. Then, I overlapped the two.

Prayer

Throughout my time of dealing with anxiety, I realized I hadn't actually asked God for help with it. I'd prayed for many things, but that wasn't one of them. I'm not sure why. I didn't always understand God's plan, but I knew he had one. I trusted Him to be with us along the way. But, that was the closest I had come to praying about my anxiety.

So, I started praying about it. Instead of just asking Him for help with my anxiety, I prayed specifically that He would help me see His goodness and presence in my life. I knew that's what I needed most.

While I am in a much better place with my anxiety right now, I still keep this prayer on my prayer list and pray it regularly.

God helped me to see His goodness and presence. He helped me to start focusing on more than on the challenges of life. And praying this way helped me to start noticing things more. I was more aware of and on the lookout for Him just like I needed to be.

A gratitude journal

At the same time, I also started keeping a gratitude journal. I challenged myself to write down at least three different things daily I was thankful for that day. I did my best to focus on smaller things for which I was grateful. For example, I didn't allow myself to list my husband and children each day.

Being intentional about looking for and finding good in each day helped me start to see the good things that were happening. I thanked God for those things after I wrote them down.

Slowly, over a month or two, my focus started shifting to the positive things and my anxiety started improving as a result. Keeping a gratitude journal played a big part.

Date: _______________________

List Three

List three simple pleasures you appreciate.

1. _______________________

____

____

2. _______________________

____

____

3. _______________________

____

____

Question

What material item(s) made your life easier today?

Today's Mood

- ◯ Happy
- ◯ Sad
- ◯ Angry
- ◯ Anxious
- ◯ Excited
- ◯ Afraid
- ◯ Lonely
- ◯ Jealous
- ◯ Calm
- ◯ Disgusted

Prayers

Date: _______________________

List three things you're thankful for right now.

1. _______________________________________

____

____

2. _______________________________________

____

____

3. _______________________________________

____

____

What did you accomplish today that makes you feel proud?

- ◯ Happy
- ◯ Sad
- ◯ Angry
- ◯ Anxious
- ◯ Excited
- ◯ Afraid
- ◯ Lonely
- ◯ Jealous
- ◯ Calm
- ◯ Disgusted

Date: _______________________

List three people who have taught you about God.

1. _______________________

2. _______________________

3. _______________________

Who has been the biggest influence on your faith? How?

◯ Happy   ◯ Afraid

◯ Sad   ◯ Lonely

◯ Angry   ◯ Jealous

◯ Anxious   ◯ Calm

◯ Excited   ◯ Disgusted

If you try to make everyone happy all the time, you won't succeed and will lose parts of yourself. And that's a shame, because the world has only one you!

3 More Prayers for Women

Emotional and mental health

"When anxiety was great within me, your consolation brought me joy." – Psalm 94:19
Lord, when I have anxiety great within, I ask that you console me and bring me joy. Strengthen me mentally and emotionally. Give my mind rest. Help me show my children what good mental healthcare looks like. Father, give me courage to seek help when I need it. Heal me from past hurt and trauma. Remind me always of your goodness and presence in my life. In Jesus' name I pray, Amen.

Relationships with others

"Therefore encourage one another and build each other up, just as in fact you are doing." – 1 Thessalonians 5:11
Heavenly Father, thank you for the loved ones you've surrounded me with. Help me to encourage and build them up. Show me how to best communicate with my husband and with my children to strengthen and grow our relationships. Please help my relationships with other people to be healthy and good for me. If someone is hurting my walk with you, help me to realize that and give me wisdom to address it. In Jesus' name I pray, Amen.

Spiritual growth

"I am the vine; you are the branches. If you remain in me and I in you, you will bear much fruit; apart from me you can do nothing." – John 15:5
Lord, I ask that you help me to remain in you and to bear much fruit. I know apart from you I can do nothing. Open my heart and mind to hear you. Help me to know you more completely. Father, remind me to connect with you during my busiest times. I want to spend time with you. Show me ways I can make that happen. In Jesus' name I pray, Amen.

Notes

List Three

List three happy moments from the day.

1. _______________________

   ____

   ____

2. _______________________

   ____

   ____

3. _______________________

   ____

   ____

Question

Describe your perfect day.

Today's Mood

- ○ Happy
- ○ Sad
- ○ Angry
- ○ Anxious
- ○ Excited
- ○ Afraid
- ○ Lonely
- ○ Jealous
- ○ Calm
- ○ Disgusted

Prayers

Date: _______________________________

List three things that made you smile today.

1. _______________________________

   ____

   ____

2. _______________________________

   ____

   ____

3. _______________________________

   ____

   ____

Where is your favorite place? Why?

○ Happy   ○ Afraid

○ Sad   ○ Lonely

○ Angry   ○ Jealous

○ Anxious   ○ Calm

○ Excited   ○ Disgusted

Date: _______________________

List three small blessings from God.

1. _______________________

____

____

2. _______________________

____

____

3. _______________________

____

____

Why is it important to appreciate all of God's gifts?

○ Happy   ○ Afraid

○ Sad   ○ Lonely

○ Angry   ○ Jealous

○ Anxious   ○ Calm

○ Excited   ○ Disgusted

Being grateful for what we have makes us happy for what we have.

5 Bible Verses to Encourage You

He replied, "Because you have so little faith. Truly I tell you, if you have faith as small as a mustard seed, you can say to this mountain, 'Move from here to there,' and it will move. Nothing will be impossible for you." – Matthew 17:20
I love this reminder of what just a teeny, tiny amount of faith can do! Have you seen a mustard seed? They are 0.1 inch in diameter! That's tiny. Jesus is telling us here that even if our faith is small, it is still powerful. Can our faith be big? Of course! But even when it isn't, it is still powerful.

"Now faith is confidence in what we hope for and assurance about what we do not see." – Hebrews 11:1
I struggle with confidence in myself. And sometimes that can influence the confidence I have in God. I can slip into a negative attitude like, "I know God can fix this, but I don't think He will." I don't usually utter those words aloud, but God hears them in my heart. This verse, though, convicts my heart. Faith is being confident in the God we serve. I can't be confident in myself and that I'll always come out on top, but I can be confident God knows what He's doing and will come out on top. I am assured and can be hopeful that no matter what life brings, God is there with me. What better description of faith is there?!

"May the God of hope fill you with all joy and peace as you trust in him, so that you may overflow with hope by the power of the Holy Spirit." – Romans 15:13
Faith and trust really do go hand-in-hand. If we have faith in God and Who He is, then we can trust He will always be with us. Not only does this verse remind us we can have faith and trust in God, but it also tells us God is a God of hope. Trusting in Him will bring us joy and peace. And, finally, it reminds us that the power of the Holy Spirit can fill our hearts to overflowing with hope.

"'Go,' said Jesus, 'your faith has healed you.' Immediately he received his sight and followed Jesus along the road." – Mark 10:52
This is one example of many in the New Testament where Jesus heals someone based on their faith. They truly believe in Him and His power. He sees our hearts and knows our faith. Does this mean we will always get what we want? No. Does it mean we will always be healed on earth? Also, no. But it does mean that God sees you and will reward your faith. It also means our faith is about following Jesus. Instead of running off to live his life in a way he'd only previously imagined, the former blind man immediately followed Jesus. He knew where his blessing and healing had come from. We, too, know where our blessings come from and can put our faith in Him!

"I have chosen the way of faithfulness; I have set my heart on your laws." – Psalm 119:30
Faithfulness is a way of life we can choose. We choose faith even when our faith is shaken and wavering. Sometimes when we go through the acts of faithfulness, it grows our faith. I have had times when my heart just wasn't into worshipping God. Yet, I found myself drawn along in worship with other believers and before I knew it, God blessed my heart and encouraged me. Living the life we know God has called us lead will draw us closer to Him, even when we are resistant or out of sorts.

Date: _______________________________

<table>
<tr><td>

List Three

List three things you like about your body.

1. _______________________________

   ____

   ____

2. _______________________________

   ____

   ____

3. _______________________________

   ____

   ____

</td><td>

Question

What did your body allow you to do today?

</td></tr>
</table>

Today's Mood

○ Happy   ○ Afraid

○ Sad   ○ Lonely

○ Angry   ○ Jealous

○ Anxious   ○ Calm

○ Excited   ○ Disgusted

Prayers

Date: _______________________

List three times you've felt God's presence.

1. _______________________

____

____

2. _______________________

____

____

3. _______________________

____

____

Where, when and how do you feel closest to God?

○ Happy   ○ Afraid

○ Sad   ○ Lonely

○ Angry   ○ Jealous

○ Anxious   ○ Calm

○ Excited   ○ Disgusted

Date: _______________________

List three people who make you laugh.

1. _______________________

____

____

2. _______________________

____

____

3. _______________________

____

____

What inspired you today? Why?

- ◯ Happy
- ◯ Sad
- ◯ Angry
- ◯ Anxious
- ◯ Excited

- ◯ Afraid
- ◯ Lonely
- ◯ Jealous
- ◯ Calm
- ◯ Disgusted

Doing the best you can doesn't
mean you have to be perfect.

5 More Bible Verses to Encourage You

"Consequently, faith comes from hearing the message, and the message is heard through the word about Christ." – Romans 10:17
I've been going to church my entire life. I cannot begin to tell you every sermon I've heard preached or Sunday School lesson I've sat through. But, they have all impacted me. They have served to grow and strengthen my faith. This verse plainly tells us that faith comes from hearing the message, which is the word of Christ. Keep on reading God's Word, meeting with His people and listening to music that focuses on Him to keep your faith in tact.

"You will keep in perfect peace those whose minds are steadfast, because they trust in you." – Isaiah 26:3
The peace in this verse is like that talked about in Philippians 4:7. It is God's peace that is beyond our understanding. When we trust in God, no matter how dire the circumstance is, He can give us peace that doesn't make any sense. He can bring us comfort and assurance through every moment.

"Those who know your name trust in you, for you, Lord, have never forsaken those who seek you." – Psalm 9:10
This is a good verse to remember for those times you feel like giving up. I love the reminder to trust in God and in HIs name because He has never left me. Remembering God's faithfulness in the past helps me have faith and trust in Him even more in the present.

"When I am afraid, I put my trust in you. In God, whose word I praise—in God I trust and am not afraid. What can mere mortals do to me?" – Psalms 56:3-4
My all-time favorite Bible verse is Isaiah 41:10, which reminds me that God is always with me and I don't have to be afraid. These verses takes that even a step further. Not only can we trust in God when we're afraid and have Him give us peace, but we can rest assured there is nothing of eternal consequence others can do to us. We sometimes need to hear the perspective that God is so much bigger than the hard times we go through.

"Trust in the Lord with all your heart and lean not on your own understanding; in all your ways submit to him, and he will make your paths straight." – Proverbs 3:5-6
Trusting in God looks like letting go of trying to make sense of things. If we are leaning on His understanding, then we are not leaning on our own. Faith and trust often don't make a lot of logical sense. As we choose to follow God, we can decide He knows what He's doing more than we can understand. Many times later on we are able to look back and see why He did things that didn't makes sense at the time.

Date: _______________________

List three places you can have alone time with God.

1. _______________________
____
____

2. _______________________
____
____

3. _______________________
____
____

When and how did you spend time with God today?

- ◯ Happy
- ◯ Sad
- ◯ Angry
- ◯ Anxious
- ◯ Excited
- ◯ Afraid
- ◯ Lonely
- ◯ Jealous
- ◯ Calm
- ◯ Disgusted

Date: _______________________________

List Three

List three people on whom you can depend.

1. ________________________________

____

____

2. ________________________________

____

____

3. ________________________________

____

____

Question

Share a favorite childhood memory.

Today's Mood

- ◯ Happy
- ◯ Sad
- ◯ Angry
- ◯ Anxious
- ◯ Excited
- ◯ Afraid
- ◯ Lonely
- ◯ Jealous
- ◯ Calm
- ◯ Disgusted

Prayers

Date: ______________________

List three challenges you have overcome.

1. _______________________________
____
____

2. _______________________________
____
____

3. _______________________________
____
____

Who made you feel loved today? How?

- ○ Happy
- ○ Sad
- ○ Angry
- ○ Anxious
- ○ Excited

- ○ Afraid
- ○ Lonely
- ○ Jealous
- ○ Calm
- ○ Disgusted

Date: ______________________________

Life is too short to stress over things that don't
matter in the long run. Instead, choose to let them
go so you have room for all the good in your life.

Be Grateful For Who You Are

Take a minute and think about the women around you. Think about what they're good at. I'd wager sometimes you feel less than in comparison. For example, I'll never be a great artist who draws personalized coloring pages for my children's birthday parties like my friend Carol does. I'm lucky to draw stick figures that even remote look like people!

I could go on and on and on. But the bottom line is, I don't have the same skillsets and natural talents as every woman I meet. Yes, I could take classes to try and learn some skills, but those aren't things I enjoy enough to do so. I don't want to spend the time, energy or resources on them.

And that's OK. I am who I am. Who I am is the woman that God made. Who I am is the woman God gave my children to. The same is true for you. None of us are identical. My strengths and passions are different from yours. It is what makes us unique people. While we know everyone should embrace their individuality, we often fail to do so. We get caught in the comparison trap.

Coming up short

Whenever we compare ourselves to others, we often come up short. We are judging their abilities at their best against our abilities at our worst. Instead we need to focus on how we love our families and serve the world. We don't want to be so caught in the comparison trap that we miss out on what matters most!

We all do things differently. Life isn't about what we do and what we're good at. It's not about being perfect and excelling at homemaking, business, crafts, baking and everything else. Life is about loving God and others. It's about showing others what God's love looks like in practice.

None of that has anything to do with your talents and hobbies or those of the women around you. You bring your own unique way to love and perspective to the table, and it's exactly as you were meant to. God didn't create you as you are on accident.

Remembering Whose opinion really matters

We need to work to be the women God created us to be, and that's it. Our measuring stick doesn't come from other women or the world. It doesn't even come from ourselves. It comes from our Heavenly Father, and I promise you He isn't finding you lacking when your fall short.

God's grace covers all your mess-ups. And His strength holds you up when you are wobbling. He created you just as you are. And THAT is definitely good enough, so stop comparing yourself to someone you weren't made to be.

A Final Note

I'm so glad you made it through this journal! I pray you found it encouraging and uplifting and it helped you on your spiritual journey.

I would love to hear your feedback. You're welcome to email me at stacey@writtencreations.com or find me on my site, FamiliesWithGrace.com. Families with Grace has content that encourages and uplifts moms while also being realistic, honest and practical.

Blessings!
Stacey A. Shannon

9 781088 171004